Praise for
Robert Cowley's thought-provoking anthologies:

What If? ™
The World's Foremost Military Historians
Imagine What Might Have Been
The New York Times Bestseller

"Fascinating and provocative."   —*The New York Times Book Review*

"Counterfactual supposes, would-haves, might-haves, could-haves, possiblys, perhaps, probablys and maybes, in all their dizzying permutations."
                                                        —*Time*

"Great fun. You'll have the vertigo-inducing sense that everything, you and me included, could have been very, very different. A."
                                                —*Entertainment Weekly*

"Tantalizing."   —*Chicago Tribune*

"Lively exercises in a fascinating game historians call 'the counterfactual.'"
                                                —*Chicago Sun-Times*

"The plausible and provocative historical fancies collected in this lively book demonstrate again and again that nothing in the past was ever inevitable."   —Geoffrey C. Ward, coauthor of *The Civil War*

"*What If?*™ shows us that . . . history is not an inevitable march of dusty names, dates and places, but a precarious, careening ride that could have taken us to any number of destinations."   —*Milwaukee Journal Sentinel*

"Masters of history and the written word . . . paint compelling portraits. These historians enjoy their forays into 'what if' history. It's fun to tag along."   —*The Christian Science Monitor*

"Treat yourself to *What If?*™ and wonder how different your life could have been."   —*Florida Today*

continued .

"Casts an intriguing glance at how one person can—and has—made a difference in the world."
　　　　　　　　　　　　　　　　　　　　　　　　—*St. Petersburg Times*

"The book of the year for any history lover."
　　　　　　　　　　　　　　　　　　　　　　　　—*Kirkus Reviews*

"Consistently well-drawn, these scenarios open intellectual as well as imaginative doors."
　　　　　　　　　　　　　　　　　　　　　　　　—*Publishers Weekly*

"A captivating display of historical imagination, *What If?* ™ takes us through 2,500 years of close squeaks and narrow misses." 　　—C. Vann Woodward,
Sterling Professor of History Emeritus, Yale University

"Pure, almost illicit pleasure. Excellent. A splendid book."
　　　　　　　　　　　　　　　　　　　　　　　　—*The Sunday Telegraph*

"One of the delights of the book is that broad speculative analysis is built from a mass of exciting detail. This makes for a top-class bedside read."
　　　　　　　　　　　　　　　　　　　　　　　　—*Financial Times* (London)

No End Save Victory
Perspectives on World War II
A Book-of-the-Month Club Main Selection
A History Book Club Alternate

"Compelling essays."
　　　　　　　　　　　　　　　　　　　　　　　　—*The Denver Post*

"Riveting."
　　　　　　　　　　　　　　　　　　　　　　　　—*Richmond Times-Dispatch*

"Compelling . . . Enlightening . . . Filled with stories of heroes and villains, momentous achievements and major defeats. . . . Each essay is complete, which makes this book a wonderful piece for episodic reading. Yet, in its piecemeal approach, the book manages to capture the grand sweep of the war and the men fighting it."
　　　　　　　　　　　　　　　　　　　　　　　　—*The Indianapolis Star*